WHY DID I BECOME A LANDLORD?

The Things You Need To Know
Before You Take That Leap Of Faith

BY

KARL WIDEMAN

Order this book online at www.trafford.com
or email orders@trafford.com

Most Trafford titles are also available at major online book retailers.

Printed in the United States of America.

ISBN: 978-1-4269-4754-4 (sc)
ISBN: 978-1-4269-4755-1 (e)

Trafford rev. 02/23/2011

 www.trafford.com

North America & international
toll-free: 1 888 232 4444 (USA & Canada)
phone: 250 383 6864 ◆ fax: 812 355 4082

ACKNOWLEDGMENTS

I would like to thank my Mother, Vivian Lampkin, for her strength and wisdom and her courage to never quit on any of her endeavors. Watching her go after what she wanted encouraged me to go after what I believed in.

I would like to also thank Sandra Coburn for her tireless help and encouragement to make this book a reality. She was there from the start of the book until it was finished.

And last but not least I would like to thank my family for always believing in me.

CONTENTS

Chapters

INTRODUCTION

The reason I decided to write this book is to give others insight into the apartment rental business. The book is designed to be informative and to serve as a how to manual. I want to share just what is involved on a daily, weekly and monthly basis, in the life of a Landlord.

It is for people that have always wondered about what's involved in owning rental property and never knew where to start. It is for those who might be considering buying a rental property now or in the near future.

It is also for the person that is already a rental property owner and would like some pointers and references, things they might not be aware of. This book will touch some of the key areas of owning rental property such as: managing, tenant screening, cost savings, security, decorating, good record keeping, do's and don'ts, just to name a few. So sit back, read and enjoy.

THE MODEL TENANT

This group of tenants makes owning rental property a pleasure. They pay their rent on time, they take pride in where they live and will go above and beyond what you expect from them. They will treat your place with respect and keep it clean and together, as if they own it. And when it's time for them to move out of your place, it will be given back to you the same way that you gave it to them. There are a lot of tenants like this. If all my tenants were like this, I wouldn't have a book to write. But in the real world it is not possible. However, if you should be lucky enough to only have model tenants, you are a very fortunate landlord. My hat goes off to this jewel of a tenant. I would like to thank you.

THE PESKY TENANT

This type of tenant is one I would try to avoid, if possible. You can never please them no matter how nice the apartment is they can always find fault with something. It is never quite right. Every time you see them, they will have something to show you or tell you about in their apartment. They want you to pick up rent payments in person just so they can complain. The red flag to look out for with this particular tenant is when they view the apartment for the very first time, they tend to take three to four times longer than the average, perspective tenant, everything is pointed out to you, and you can watch their facial expressions to see that they are not happy with the place, but they will rent it anyway. After you agree to rent to them things don't get better they get worse. Now you are hearing complaints twenty-four seven. What I have tried to explain to this particular tenant is that if I go home and look for things that are not perfect, I will find them, even on high end rentals. They will shake their heads in agreement, and return to complaining anyway.

If you happen to rent to someone like this, you have to draw the line in the sand and decide how far to go and maybe offer only a six-month lease or a month-to-month tenancy basis. This way if it's not working, you can ask for the apartment back and not be stuck for twelve months at a time. Each time I rent to someone like this I regret it. Most of the time tenants like this either have a lot of time on their hands or don't have money coming in on a regular basis to pay their rent. Again avoid this type of tenant, if possible.

DO'S AND DON'TS

Landlords and Property Managers have a moral obligation to conduct themselves in a professional manner at all times. For instance they should never engage in personal relationships with the tenant because it can blur the lines between what remains business and what becomes personal. It can interfere with the rent being paid on time or paid at all. Respect could be lost and the rules of the building could be broken. It's just not a winning situation for the landlord.

Family members can pose the same problems or worse, if the rent is $800 dollars per month, family members want to know how much do I have to pay, of course they are expecting a generous reduction, if they can't pay the full rent, they do expect you to just understand. It can also damage family relationships if they don't work out as a tenant, and you ask them to move.

Never discuss with a tenant problems you are having with another tenant. Also never discuss with other tenants those that are paying on time or who is not paying.

Whenever a tenant offers to help out around the property, i.e., cutting grass, shoveling snow, cleaning stairwells, etc. keep these things strictly business and pay the tenant. This will stop any suggestions of reduction in rent payments, or mention of what they have done for you, when they are unable to pay their rent.

JOYS AND BENEFITS OF RENTAL PROPERTIES

It is a proud feeling to own rental property. When you look at the structure and say to yourself, this is mine, unlike renting you pay your rent for twelve months and all you get is a place to live. Ownership means you make all the decisions on how you want things to be, you don't go by the rules, you make the rules and if your tenants are paying you and the monies received are over your expenses, you are also making a profit while tenant rent payments are paying the mortgage on the rental property.

I have a rule of thumb, let's say you purchased a property in a decent area at a decent price, in years the property value will double the value of what you paid for it. Also as an owner you are not paying month-to-month without any personal gain, as renters do, you are accruing equity. Did I mention the deductions at tax time, every repair, upgrade, etc. is a tax deduction for you at the end of the year.

If you live in your rental property, the Internal Revenue Service will give you a percentage deduction as well. Note: Always check with a professional. If all goes well at your rental properties, you can get depreciation and appreciation and more when tenants are paying, in real estate, it can be a great investment. Rental properties can be a part of your investment portfolio, as always check with a Financial Planner for investment tips.

ADVANTAGES OF LIVING IN YOUR RENTAL PROPERTY

ADVANTAGES:

- The tenant or tenant's help you with the expenses of where you live
- You see what's going on, on a daily basis at your property

DISADVANTAGES:

- You are too accessible to tenants' all hours of the day.
- If you are sensitive to every little thing, I would not suggest living in the rental property with tenants
- If you are sensitive to noise, someone above or below you won't make you happy.

I would suggest having a separate residence away from your tenants so that you have your own yard and private time for yourself. I have also noticed that when you don't live in your rental property, you get fewer complaints and requests. And you are not constantly seeing who is coming and going. My advice is to live in your rental property until you are able to have a separate residence. You will thank me later.

LOCATION, LOCATION, LOCATION

When choosing where to buy property consider these things:

- Always buy property that you would be willing to live in, because there might come a time that you will have to move into this property. (i.e. to protect your investment).
- Buy close to transportation lines. The perspective tenant might not drive or have a car.
- Don't buy on a deserted block or dimly lit block.
- Don't buy on a block with obvious drug or other undesirable activity present.
- Don't buy on a block with a lot of people hanging out on the corners. It can be discouraging to your perspective tenant.
- Don't buy in an area close to a liquor store.
- Don't buy in an area where neighbors appear to not care about keeping the area clean.
- Try to buy in an area that is up and coming

BUYING PROPERTY TO REHAB OR ONE THAT IS IN DECENT CONDITION

When buying your first rental property, you may be tempted to buy a fixer upper. By that I mean one to rehab. Here are the pros and cons of rehabing a property. Pro is that you will probably get it at a good price. The Con is you have to fix it up. When you buy a rehab property you might get lucky and only have to do some minor repairs but in most cases there is a lot to be done, i.e., plumbing, drywall, electrical, flooring, roofing, exterior work, carpentry, etc. Unless you are skilled in these areas, you will have to hire someone to do it for you, which can be costly. If you are new at this, and don't forget while you are getting it ready to be rented out, you have your other expenses too, like the mortgage, insurance, taxes, utilities and someone to watch the property to protect against vandalism and theft. My advice is to buy a property ready to be rented out with everything in working condition. This way if you do have to do anything, it will be minimal. Make sure that the roof is in decent shape and that there is no major repairs to do once you buy the property. There will be some expenses i.e., changing locks or re-keying them that you should plan for. If you do not know how to change locks, check with your local locksmith or hardware store. Never let a property sit empty for an extended period of time. Be ready to rent it out as soon as possible and if you need advice on the condition of a property, have a certified inspector check it out for you. This is another expense that should be factored into the cost of buying a property. Good luck with your purchase.

HOW MUCH TO SPEND ON RENTAL PROPERTY

When buying an investment property, it doesn't matter if it costs one dollar or one million dollars; it depends on what you can afford and what you are comfortable with as far as expenses. Some of your monthly expenses will be:

1) Mortgage
2) Taxes
3) Insurance
4) Water Bill
5) Gas Bill (Heat & Hot Water)
6) Light Bill (Common area lights on the outside of the building)
7) Extermination (If needed)
8) Percentage for repairs
9) Percentage of money set aside for & emergencies
10) Percentage of at least two to three-month's mortgages set aside

These are monthly recurring expenses. You want to buy a property where after all expenses are paid you either make a profit or break even. It is never good to buy a property that won't generate income because the whole idea is to supplement your income and add to it. If the property is draining your resources, the asset has now become a liability. Always remember assets put money in your pocket. Liabilities take money out of your pocket. Now don't get me wrong, from time to time you will have to do it. Let's say if a tenant moves out of your single family house, 100% of your income is lost and you will be responsible for all expenses at that property not to mention possibly every day or every other day checking on your investment. On the other hand if you own a two flat or more, you will still have income coming in and the property won't be sitting vacant. In a worse case scenario, let's say you had a tenant that was renting your house and for whatever reason couldn't pay the rent anymore, or was causing problems for the house and you decide that the tenant has to go. When you tell the tenant that you will no longer rent to him or her and they refuse to leave in the allotted time you give them, you now have to put them in eviction court. This can be a very time consuming and costly. While you are waiting for the time to pass that the court gives them to vacate, the tenant could be destroying your house. They could let the water run day and night with stoppers in letting water run throughout the house damaging the carpet, buckling wood floors and damaging the ceilings below. All you can do is wait for them to leave or be set out.

One of my fellow landlords had this to happen to him and when I saw the house it looked like someone had blown the place up with a bomb. It wasn't pretty. Now if this happens in a multi-unit building, somebody will notice water coming into their apartment and you would be notified before too much damage occurs. One of the things that I always do when I have the unpleasant task of putting a tenant out is not to argue with them, because they are already upset with you. So, you want to ease a person out while they are in the process of moving out with the least amount of tension possible. Remember some people can be very spiteful, even if they are in the wrong. So, just brace yourself for the worse and hope for the best. I have to say that not all tenants are like this. Some will clean the place and maybe even paint. I personally prefer them not to paint. If the job is messy, it can cost you more to get the place ready for the next tenant. Therefore cleaning the apartment is sufficient for me. Never use your personal funds to save or operate a building. A building must survive on its own. Also never use your personal residence as collateral, because if the rental property is in trouble, you could lose your home.

ADVANTAGES OF A FLAT ROOF VERSUS A PITCH ROOF

The advantage of having a flat roof as opposed to a pitch roof is enormous. If you are not afraid to climb a ladder up the back or side of the building to get to the roof, or go through a roof hatch on the back porch, then you are pretty much home free. But a word of caution, anything high up should be taken seriously because if you are not careful you can fall off. If you feel that you are up to the task, you can patch the roof for leaks, and do preventive maintenance to prevent future problems. Check with your local building supply house for any and all supplies needed.

Now on to the pitch roof. I would not recommend buying a property with a pitch roof. If there is roof work needed, working on a pitch roof can be very dangerous, and you can easily fall off. In my life time I've worked on two. Once on my single story home, which was tricky and then once on my two story apartment building. It was very dangerous as well as "scary as heck." The reason I worked on them both was to save money. But what I should have looked at were the dangers involved. What if I had fallen off the roof? I could have been seriously injured leaving me unable to go to work and in most cases not able to work around the properties, too. So, if you look at it from this stand point, it would have made better sense to have a professional roofer work on the two properties.

So the bottom line is a flat roof, is the safest to work on. You can make most repairs yourself. You can also roll on silver paint to reflect the sun and keep the building cooler.

Word of Caution: If For Any Reason You Don't Feel Comfortable, Let a Professional Do The Work. They should be licensed, bonded and insured. This way you won't be sued if someone hurts themselves on Your Property.

SECURING YOUR RENTAL PROPERTY

Security of the property is another important part of owning a rental property, this is an area I take very seriously a well-lit building or house can deter a possible break in or robbery. Now days you can buy the low wattage bulbs which will save you a lot of money. I use sensors on my rental properties as well as my personal residence. You can either buy them already connected to your outside light fixtures or add them to your existing fixtures. There are different types of sensors to purchase, like the motion detector which turns on the lights once it senses or picks up any movement. Then you have my favorite type of sensor that comes on when it starts to get dark and it goes off when the sun comes up again. The way sensor's work is not only do they turn on the porch light they also turn on hallway lights too. This way you don't have to rely on the tenants to turn them on and off.

There will be times when one of your tenants will move out or both, in the case of a two flat building you will have to deal with keeping the building secure until you find new tenants. Here is my strategy for dealing with this issue. If you have a house that you are renting and the tenant moves out, the very 1st thing you should do is re-key the locks. You will notice that I didn't say change the locks. There are two ways that you can do this. You can take the cylinder of the lock to a locksmith and have him or her re-key your locks at $14 or more or you can invest in a lock re-pinning kit that you can buy on the internet or a locksmith store along with the book on how to re-key or re-pin locks. I do my own on-sight this way it is done and over.

Once I secure my lock's I then inspect for vulnerable areas where it would be easy for someone to break in and secure those areas. Now that I have the lights coming on in the front and back of the property, I then make sure that the property still looks lived in, as much as possible, by leaving the key areas of the house lit, it doesn't hurt to have a TV on a timer going on near the main front window. The TV gives off its own reflection and it is as if someone is there watching TV. There should be a light in the same room but on a different timer. This gives the impression that the person got up to turn the light off at some point. Next, you want to go by your property at least once a day to check the locks, door's, windows, etc. I generally check my properties when they are vacant at least twice a day. If it's in the winter time and it is snowing, you want to make sure to shovel the snow. Because you don't have anyone living there, you may feel this is not a priority however you should keep in mind that people do notice if it is not being done. If it is spring or summer you should make sure to keep leaves raked and clean up around the property on a regular basis. This will let people know that someone is watching the property.

I can remember when I bought my first property, I lived on the other side of town and while I was getting it ready on the weekends which was the only time I was checking the place, this one particular time I decided to drive out to the property, when I got there the side gate was open and the back door to the building was opened too. **Stop: Word of advice, never go into your property if it looks like someone has broken in because they might still be inside and you could walk in on them and they could seriously injure or kill you!** Always go to a safe area and call the Police then let the police do their job. Always make sure that you thank them for putting their lives on the line. At the time I didn't know any better and the first thing that I did was walk throughout the whole building by myself. Thank God no one was in the building.

However, they left some of their tools, like a pipe wrench for the radiators. So, I had to immediately secure the place and live there while I was getting it ready to be rented out. I'm not a big fan of posting a "For Rent" sign on the front of the property because it lets everybody know that you have an empty apartment or two and it can bring unwanted, oftentimes negative attention or activity to the property. I like to place an ad in the newspaper this way the only people coming to the property are those that need an apartment or house to rent. This eliminates those that are coming by the property to check it out only to come back later to burglarize it.

I had a two-flat that was vacant for almost eleven months. I had fallen behind on the mortgage because both tenants had stopped paying rent. The bank was threatening to foreclose on the property but I still took care of the place. I would check it in the morning as well as when I got off work. This one particular day, the same as usual, my girlfriend and I pulled up to the back of the building 1st to inspect to see if anything was out of place, and this time it was. I normally place the garbage cans next to the gate, but I noticed that they had been moved. So, as I went into the yard, I heard a loud bumping sound as I got closer to the building I noticed that the outer basement door had been kicked down also the 1st floor apartment back door was standing open. I went back to the car, drove across the street from the building and called 911 for the police. We then waited for them to arrive. When they finally arrived, the Police went in and came out with two teenagers one 14 and the other 16 years' old. They both lived in the neighborhood. When the Police put them in the back of the squad car, we went down to the basement; water was running from damaged pipes, water was everywhere. The thieves had cut all my copper piping to take to the scrap yard for pennies on the dollar, which on the other hand cost me money to replace. Not only the copper piping had to be replaced but two first floor doors and the door leading to the basement had to be replaced. Had I not been checking on the property regularly, a lot more damage would have been done. They could have vandalized the whole building, when both apartments were ready to rent out. Thank goodness I had some knowledge on how to do some plumbing because I would have had to call a plumber to replace the copper piping and a carpenter to replace the doors and frames.

As for the two young men that broke into the property, the 14-year-old received a month in Juvenile Hall and the 16-year-old, I believe was sent to county jail. So, if you have vacant property and you cannot afford to hire someone to watch it for you, you become that someone.

It is also a good idea to have a house-sitter, someone who can live in the property until you rent it out. I have an Attorney friend who bought a six-flat building. He thought it was okay to just check on it occasionally. One evening he went by the building, and to his amazement, homeless people had set up camp in his building. When he called the Police to have them removed, they told the Police that they lived there. So the officer told my friend that there was nothing that he could do, he would have to put them through Eviction Court to have them removed from the property. However, my friend just had someone to watch and wait for them to leave the building, he secured it so they could not return, and kept a daily watch on the property from then on. Imagine having to put someone in Eviction Court that you don't know, you never rented to, it's expensive and crazy!

GETTING APARTMENTS READY TO RENT

When getting an apartment ready to rent before you begin decorating, keep three things in mind: The carpet, the walls, the floor tiles. These are the basics of apartment readiness and the least expensive way to go if you are on a budget with a limited amount of cash to work with.

If you need cabinets for the kitchen, buy the ones that are in stock as opposed to specialty items. They generally cost less; follow the same rule if counter tops need to be replaced. I generally buy the same paint color, usually off-white, like an antique white in a flat finish and semi-gloss; normally I paint all rooms in the flat finish and use the semi-gloss in the kitchen and bathroom. What is great about using flat paint is that it is easy to touch up areas plus it hides imperfections in the wall. There may be times when you have to use a primer. I recommend one with no odor like the Kilz brand. Primer is good for covering over areas on the walls where it would only bleed through the paint. You would first use the primer then one coat of paint. If there are small holes in the wall, use some spackle then lightly sand it. Then apply your primer and paint. If you have to replace interior doors, I would recommend solid core doors as opposed to hollow core doors. Solid core doors are all wood. The hollow core doors have a thin skin of wood on the outside and a paper product on the inside. It is a cheaper door, but if you add up how many doors you will go through, it would have made sense to spend the higher cost up front and get a better, solid core door. If the money isn't there to buy carpet or to put down wood floors, which will require sanding then staining, and after that sealing with polyurethane, I would recommend buying some dark brown gloss or semi-gloss floor paint. It looks very nice, but if you have carpet that is still in good shape and you can get away with cleaning it, I would say go for it.

The best way to make sure that every room is clean and functioning is to take a note pad and go through every room and take notes of everything that needs to be replaced, repaired or cleaned. Then make a note of the materials you will need. Before you purchase new materials, check your inventory to see if you already have some of the materials in stock. This will save you money and shopping time.

Remember that first impressions count. When people first approach the property, the first thing they look at is how the property is being maintained, i.e. if there is a lot of paper or garbage, broken windows, how secure is the property, does it look clean, is the grass cut, are people hanging out on the front of neighboring properties? I make it a point to always keep the property looking neat and clean. Think about it, if the outside looks bad, do you really want to see the inside? I have so much confidence in the appearance of my property that I suggest to the perspective tenant to drive by first to see if they like the area and the property. Then we set up a time to see the inside. In the spring and summer the grass should be cut and flowers planted. These are good selling points. In the winter the snow should be shoveled. This shows that the owner cares about his or her place. It doesn't hurt to spruce up your place every other year or as often as needed. Remember paint does wonders!

USING AGENCIES OR NOT

Using an agency might sound like an easy way to guarantee getting your rent every month, but you are getting more than you bargain for. Most likely if the average tenant is going through some type of agency they can't afford to rent from you. This would be Red Flag Number One. And what happens when the agency has paid their portion and it is time for the tenant to start paying the rent? This would be Red Flag Number Two.

This happened to me. The agency promised me six months of rent to let their Client move into my apartment. Once the tenant was in, two weeks later, the Representative that I was dealing with, prior to the tenant moving in, was fired. The new Agency Representative informed me that they were not going to pay six months rent for the tenant but two. The Agency took their time cutting me a check. Therefore I had a tenant that they vowed to help with six month's of rent payments and neither has paid me a dime. They encouraged the tenant to find a job and informed her that they would only be paying for two month's rent.

However, now I'm stuck with a tenant that would not have qualified on their own, wondering how that person will pay rent without a job. And thinking about how it's going to cost me, once again, time and money will be spent to put that person out.

Then there was a time when an Agency came to me asking me to rent an apartment to an eighteen-year-old kid. They were asking me to give him a chance to have his own apartment, while in school. They promised me if I had any problems, the Agency was just a phone call away. They would resolve any issues that might come up. However, when the young man started acting out, all I got was an answering machine no matter what time I called. In the end the Agency removed the young man from the apartment and never paid me for the damages done to the apartment. There were damages not covered by the security deposit.

My advice to perspective Landlords is to know what you are getting yourself into. Agencies are good at painting a pretty picture for their Clients until they move in then they are your problem.

TENANT SCREENING

Tenant screening is one of the most important parts of the rental business because it involves picking the best tenant possible. In some cases it will determine whether you keep your property or lose it. Most rental property owners are regular people with average jobs trying to supplement their income. So if you have a two flat or a single family home, and you are renting out to tenants that stop paying rent, you as the owner will have to start paying and this can drain you of most or all of your personal finances. And if you are like most people you are living from pay check to pay check and one pay check from living on the street. As I stated earlier, it comes down to keeping your property or losing your property due to one bad tenant decision.

I speak from experience I have been burned! I had this one perspective tenant who would come every day while I was showing the apartment. She was pleasant, kind, patient, and not to mention "kind on the eyes." There were "red flags" everywhere. I just wasn't doing what I should have. I ignored them all. For example if someone comes to you and the rent is $500.00 per month and the Daughter is working part-time at a fast-food restaurant and the perspective tenant only has income of $500.00 per month, this is evidence that they will struggle in maintaining the rent, etc. In this particular apartment, tenants' were responsible for paying their own utilities. This is a good thing, but I will get into that in the chapter on Savings and Expenses. What I should have done were the basic calculations. If their total combined income was $750.00 before they paid rent, it would leave them with $200.00 to cover all other expenses. So, if you paid for your own heat and hot water plus lights, food, etc., it would leave you with nothing to live off. What happened in this particular case, she started falling behind, and when the tenant lost her job, she could never catch herself back up on the rent. So she just stopped paying which made me fall behind on my obligation to the mortgage holder. When I had to ask her to leave, I learned that she knew the court system and she worked the system to her advantage by getting an attorney representing Better Housing for Tenants. Her representation was free while I had to hire an attorney for about $1,200.00. It turned into a long drawn out process and since the tenant didn't work she just hopped on the train and came to court watching her attorney fight for her. I had to get permission to take off work two hours every week for six months. Thank goodness I had an understanding boss and company or I would have been in bad shape. So, for six months the tenant was living rent free even after the courts ordered her to start paying, as the trial went on, she never did. Finally she moved on. Later I found out in the last seven years that she has been evicted seven times. The moral of the story is do your homework. Never rent to anyone without doing a thorough check of their rental history. We will get into the steps for checking on a perspective tenant later.

First let me say this, never assume because the person is working and you have a good business relationship with them that you don't have to do your homework. I had an excellent working relationship with a tenant that worked for my property insurance company. Anything I needed she was "Johnny on the spot" to get the job done. So when she came to me asking if I had a vacancy I thought this was a slam dunk, a no brainier, I just knew without a shadow of doubt, and without doing my homework, that this would work out.

Red Flag #1: Six months earlier she wanted to rent an apartment from me, she came out to look at the apartment but she never followed up. So, I called her and she said that she had rented another apartment instead. Six months later she calls me out of the blue, just as nice and personable as ever, and wanted to know, again, if I had an apartment that she could rent.

Red Flag #2: The 1st time around she was living with her mother and her mother wanted her out of her place ASAP! What parent would want you out ASAP unless there was a problem?

Red Flag #3: When she came back to me we talked about how much money she would need to move in. She told me that she wasn't able to pay anything up front because she lost her job but she had been approved for unemployment. So, she asked me to trust her to do the right thing. Once she moved in with no money changing hands, my business instinct kicked in and I told her I wasn't able to do it because if she didn't pay I would get burned. So, she put the guilt trip on me on how I always tried to help people and she needed help. So against my better judgment I went along with it and in the end I lost three months worth of rent and incurred court costs and two thousand dollars worth of damages to the apartment, all because I didn't do my homework.

I once rented to a kid, 18 years old. He had never rented an apartment. He was a ward of the State. He came out when I was showing an apartment. I had a couple of perspective tenant's checking out the apartment so as he started asking questions about the apartment I did not take him seriously. I felt that he was too young and inexperienced. He had his

Counselor call me and this guy was a great salesman. He told me everything that I wanted to hear. He told me how great this guy was and how he was getting good grades in school and how responsible he was within their group home. He said if I rented to him that he, the Counselor, would be only a phone call away and as for the money, it would come before the 1st of each month. It sounded like another win, win situation, so I thought. Well the agency moved him in, I got my money and everything was going smooth, so far. When the tenant moved in, it was winter so that meant that he needed heat and at this particular building tenants' were responsible for heating the apartment themselves. I told the new tenant that he had to put the gas service in his name because it was presently in my name. I worked with him and gave him a certain amount of time to put the service in his name. A month went by and the gas as well as the lights were still in my name. I tried calling his Counselor and he assured me that he would talk to the tenant. But after a month and a half I had the utilities taken out of my name and faxed the agency the bill. Some time went by and the gas company shut off the service. Now he was living in a cold apartment and he was very upset. I was at work almost ready to get off when my tenant's started calling me to let me know that the Police had been at the building looking for me. I started to worry and I thought what could I have done? To keep from being embarrassed and getting arrested on the job or on the street, I decided to go to the nearest police station and find out what was going on. When I got to the station the Sergeant looked into it but he didn't see anything in the system. He asked me if I had been having problems with anyone. I said not to my knowledge. Then I paused for a second and concluded that the teenage tenant in my building might be the issue. So, I was told to check with the police station near my house. I thanked the Sergeant and went on my way. When I arrived at my neighborhood station, the desk Sergeant there could not find anything on me either. Now I am wondering who it could be and what did they want. Early Saturday morning the door bell rings and it was a Female Detective. I let her in and found out she was a server for the City.

She served me with a citation to go to violations court because one of my tenant's, the teenager, called the City, the Department of Children and Family Services and anyone else that he could think of to complain that I wasn't supplying him with any heat. When I explained the situation to the server, she just said go to court and explain it to the Judge. So, I contacted the Counselor representing the teenager and explained what had happened. He faxed me a letter to take with me to court.

Once I was in court, the Judge dismissed the case against me. For the next two months the tenant refused to talk to the utility companies about putting the services in his name and therefore he went the remainder of winter without heat. When I asked him why he would not do it, he said because he was mad at me and I thought that was a strange way of getting back at me by freezing himself. He then started to do things to aggravate me, like running water in the kitchen and bathroom sinks with the stoppers in and letting the water overflow down to the 1st floor apartment. Then there was a fight in his apartment and the bathroom sink and a medicine cabinet was broken. There was also a broken living room window. I faxed the agency a bill with pictures, at their request however, I was never reimbursed for the damages. So I asked them to remove the tenant from the apartment, and they did. I made several follow-up calls to the agency and the Counselor never returned my calls. Remember he told me "he was only a phone call away." The only reason he started returning my calls is because I was getting on the Receptionists nerves and she gave me the Company President's phone number. After calling the President directly, explaining what was going on, he assured me he would get to the bottom of the situation and he did. Another lesson learned.

WHAT TO LOOK FOR AND REQUIRE

- Proof of Income
- Eviction Check
- Tenants must have an apartment already
- Tenants must have utility bills in their name with matching addresses
- Inspection of tenants' present apartment
- Meet everyone that will be occupying the apartment
- Get a reference from the present Landlord
- Get past rent receipts, if possible.

RED FLAGS

- No proof of income or employment
- Present Landlord is losing the building (in most cases it is due to tenants' not paying rent)
- Tenants living with someone else
- Eviction(s) showing up on the Eviction Report
- Tenant gets paid in cash
- Tenant wants to use a typed letter as proof of employment and Income Source

RENTING TO SOMEONE WITH A PAST FORECLOSURE HISTORY

This particular, perspective, tenant you have to really look at before you rent your house to them. When you interview this perspective tenant, they will tell you about their experience living in and maintaining the house they just lost, and what they can do to help maintain your house. This sounds like a slam dunk right? You are thinking to your self all that you have to do is collect the rent and they will maintain your property like it was their own. The one thing you should be asking yourself and them is how did they lose their house and if possible, you want to see proof in a documented form. The reason you want to review their history is because the same reason they lost their property could end up how they help you to lose your house, especially if it is due to none payment of the mortgage.

I had two tenants like that, they were good at fixing up the outside as well as the inside, however, when it came to being responsible with paying the rent that was an area that they were not so responsible. That is probably why they lost their houses. When you rent out a house and the tenant falls behind on the rent you lose 100% of the income from that property and guess who has to start paying the mortgage, taxes, insurance, water, etc.? You do. And if you let them go past two months, it almost, in most cases, it will be impossible to catch up. You risk losing the property as I did because I wasn't able to pay the expenses at my house as well as the expenses at the rental home.

I personally don't like houses as rental property because if a tenant is unable to pay their rent you incur 100% loss of income. The owner of the rental property next to mine decided she only cared about collecting rent payments and therefore was not selective in who she rented to. After six months the tenants started doing everything from having a lot of company to opening their home up as a gang member hang out. The front and rear yards were in disarray, drugs were being used, etc. and it did not take long for the townhouse to fall down. When the owner told them that they had to move, they completely destroyed the place. Again it is easy to put tenants in but hard as hell to get them out. Remember when perspective tenants are interviewing to rent from you they can be some of the best actors and actresses they need to be to get in. Once in, they become your problem and your nightmare, if you didn't do your homework, as in checking job references, their proof of income, past addresses and landlord, eviction and foreclosure checks. Now days you should also do a criminal background check. These are checks that can save you thousands of dollars, even if it's a family member or a friend, do your checks, you will thank me later.

RULES OF THE BUILDING

STATING THE RULES UP FRONT

This subject I like to talk about with a perspective tenant. If they are considering renting from me, we need to talk about what they can expect from me and what I expect from them. For instance if no pets are allowed I would state that, if I do not want tenants congregating on the front of the property I should state this. The rules for hanging out in the back of the building should also be clearly stated. Rules concerning loud music, if it should be turned down after a certain time and getting permission to host parties at the building, should all be explained before a tenant moves in to the building.

What the tenant can expect from the landlord should be a clean apartment and a well run building. If any repairs are needed I will get back to them in a timely manner. If tenants have any concerns I will address them. This helps because the last thing you want to hear is I wish I had known, I probably would not have rented your place. So put everything up front, in a nice way. This way they know what is expected of them as a tenant and they also know what they can expect from you as their landlord.

BENDING THE RULES

It is generally not good to bend your own rules, say for instance if you don't allow pets and you allow one tenant to have a small dog or a cat, then it won't be fair to tell the other tenants he or she is not allowed to have a pet. Or if you have the building exterminated on a regular basis and the tenant would prefer to exterminate their own apartment, I would not start this type of pattern, because it will throw the whole system of the building off. I tried that one year at my two flat and the deal was I would supply materials as needed, bad idea! One tenant was exterminating sometimes while others were not. It cost me more money as well as an even more infested building. Now it is mandatory to have all apartments sprayed no matter what and it is a good idea to inspect the apartment's at least once a year. The minute you notice a tenant going away from the rules, bring it to their attention. Remember if you let the little things slide, they will eventually turn into big things.

WAIVING LATE FEES

I had a habit of feeling bad about charging late fees especially if the tenant had a good excuse for being late with their rent payment. I had this one particular tenant that started to be late on a regular basis. And every time she had an excuse. Her Uncle died, her check was short, the car broke down, etc. I had another tenant that ran late all the time and he would give me a different reason why he was late, each time, and I would waive the fees until one day I went to do a repair at the tenant's apartment that usually had all the excuses and to my amazement I saw why she couldn't pay her rent on time, it was because she was using her money to keep her style up-to-date., i.e. the latest hair styles and wearing the latest fashions. She even went as far as buying a car. Don't get me wrong I am not knocking a person for keeping themselves together or needing and getting transportation however, priorities have to be in order and having a place to stay should be #1.

So the moral of the story is always charge your late fees and collect it. Because if you are late with the mortgage, the bank will definitely charge you a late fee.

The same goes for the Electric, Water & Gas companies. They all expect their money and so should you. No company will absorb the cost of doing business with the public they pass it on to the consumer. When I hear tenants from other rental properties say that they don't believe in rent increases I ask myself how those landlords keep up with the cost of everything going up, the costs of running a rental property. Like insurance, taxes, lights, gas, etc. I feel landlords should always give a increase even if it is modest just to get their tenants used to getting an increase.

Once a tenant was giving me the reason that he did not have his rent money, over the phone, and after awhile I heard him laughing. What I couldn't figure out was what was so funny, I wasn't telling any jokes, what was funny was I was being too nice and the tenant took it as a weakness. Even if it is not in you to be firm, you have to be, just take a deep breath and do it. Believe me it works and you will be respected.

SECURITY DEPOSITS OR NOT?

Security deposits should be used when a tenant moves out of your rental property. When a tenant moves out you can deduct, from the security deposit, for any damages done to the rental unit. It should be put in a separate bank account. Upon moving out the tenant would get the security deposit minus the costs for any damages to the apartment unit. **Caution: If you don't plan on putting the money in a special account, from day one you risk the possibility of ending up in eviction court with that tenant and having the judge ask about the security deposit, and whether or not it is in an interest bearing account.** This interest should accrue from the first day the tenant moves into the apartment. The judge can order you to pay up to three month's rent for that one month payment if your are not in compliance. What I have noticed, over the years is if you are unable to put the money in an interest bearing account don't collect a security deposit from your tenants. What you might want to do, (always check with your local government first), is collect the first and last months rent instead. This way when the tenant decides that they will be moving out they won't have to pay the final month rent. Always put everything in writing, getting all necessary signatures. When in doubt get professional advice from your local government or an attorney.

HANDING OVER THE KEYS
HAVING TENANTS SIGN
PICTURES

This is a step that I feel most landlords miss during the process of handing over the keys to their rental properties. Before giving the new tenant keys to an apartment a walk-through should be done of the entire apartment. There should be an initial walk-through, where tenants have the opportunity to request certain things be corrected (within reason) and then a final walk-through with the landlord to make sure everything is in order. Taking notes will help the landlord when the final walk-through is done. I suggest taking pictures of each room, the front and back entrances and porches. Have tenants sign off on each picture and give the tenant a copy of any notes taken on final walk-through. This will help you in two ways:

1) If there are any complaints you have pictures of the way the apartment looked upon the tenant moving in.
2) If you ever have to appear in court, you will have pictures to show the judge of what the apartment looked like when the tenant moved in, and the pictures can also be used when advertising for new renters. I feel the walk through, taking notes, and receiving tenant approval, by their signature, is needed.

COLLECTING RENT PAYMENTS

Collecting rents is one of the things necessary to survive, how else can you make a profit or pay the bills. Sure you can be understanding of your tenant's circumstances but will your creditor's be so understanding. That was me, Mr. Nice Guy, being understanding and forgiving late fees but at the end of the day I was paying late fees, going into my own pocket to pay the bills, etc. And that is not good business! You can still be a nice person but firm when it comes down to collecting the rent, you have to be almost like a bill collector. If the rent is due on the first, with a five-day grace period after the fifth day, you go to the P. O. Box to see who has paid rent, if everyone has paid, that's good. However, whoever did not pay should receive a letter, immediately, stating the amount of rent past due, along with the late fee that applies. By the 15th you should mail out another letter or send a text flagged urgent, and then if you still don't get a response, issue a five-day notice. Never get in the habit of accepting partial payments, you will find yourself getting partial payments all the time.

I have had tenants who owed me close to a thousand dollars or more wanting to give me one hundred dollars on their balance. My advice is never start accepting partial payments because this is how you will be getting future rent payments. You don't want to seem desperate for whatever amount of money they want to give you. Remember, they will be laughing at you behind your back and telling others how they got over on you. You should get tenants in the habit of regular rent increases. I also suggest, if you can, do not pick up rent payments in person for two important reasons:

Reason #1: Your safety. You don't want people to know that you are walking around with cash or checks on you because some people will set you up to be robbed. For example, I had a tenant ask me to stop by to pick up her rent when I got off work. She wanted me to come to the back of the building instead of the front door. I thought that was kind of odd because she had never asked that before. So, what I did was not call first, I just went directly over and knocked on the front door of the apartment. When she found out it was me at the door, I could hear her telling someone inside "He came to the front door instead", and when she opened the door, she asked why I hadn't called first and why I didn't come to the back door? I told her it was easier for me to come to the front, she handed me the cash and I was on my way. This is what I think would have happened had I went to the back, she would have paid me the rent that she borrowed from someone else, and when I came out to the alley someone would be waiting to rob me and take the rent I had just collected. Now, the tenant has paid rent and the person that fronted her the money, got their money back too. I never accept cash rent payments it has to be in a money order. I have also had my share of bounced personal checks. If people suspect that you have money or checks on you, they will follow you home and do a home invasion, demanding you give them the money you collected, while attacking you and family members, possibly killing you all. I know this sounds terrible, but this is a reality that we must guard ourselves from.

Having a P.O. box set up for tenants to mail rent payments to much safer. You can go to the P. O. Box anytime you want and not worry about being robbed or followed. I also feel that you should never go around dressed up or driving a fancy car because tenants will think that you don't need their rent payments.

Reason #2: Another reason I feel you should not collect rent payments in person is that tenant's will use that time as an opportunity to show you things that they feel you should fix, things that you have not heard one complaint about before it's time to collect the rent. The old saying goes "Out of sight our of mind"

THINGS TO EXPECT

When owning rental property don't expect things to go as smooth as it does at your place of residence. Following are some of the things to expect:

1) Things getting broken from time to time, in the apartment as well as on the outside of the building.

2) People are going to be late with rent around the holidays like Christmas, 4th of July, Memorial Day, etc., some tenants will be late all the time.

3) Look to paint inside the apartments every year or every other year. You will need to refresh the hallways, porches and around the building as well.

4) Expect to be a referee or peace maker between tenants.

5) Expect some of your tenants to be confrontational when you don't renew their lease or are in the process of putting them out.

6) Expect people to trash the apartment when they finally move out, we as landlords have an obligation to the tenant and that is to give them a clean, freshly painted apartment, with new or decent floor tiles and or carpet, working faucets, etc. What I have noticed is that some or most tenants are critical of the apartments when looking to move in, however upon moving they leave the apartment in the worst possible condition (i.e., nasty, filthy, stoves & refrigerators in such bad condition I could only throw them out). I have also

had tenants that leave the apartment as clean and in the same condition that you gave it to them.

7) Don't expect some tenants to appreciate you going out of your way for them, when it comes down to scheduling work around them being available or when you don't charge for something they clearly broke or damaged, that clearly costs you time and money. You should also not expect appreciation for not giving rent increases every year.

8) Expect to work more around your rental property than you do at your own home.

9) Expect to be juggling your money to keep everything up and running.

10) Expect to be going to Eviction Court spending money on court costs and possibly Attorney fees from time to time.

11) Expect to lose money due to non-payments from tenants.

12) Expect spiteful tenants to call the City on you for violations within and outside of your rental property (even though it is hard to make repairs when you are not receiving any rent payments), and this can be very expensive.

SERVICE CALLS

Service calls are part of being a landlord. From time to time you will be getting calls about the sink or toilet being clogged or both, the light doesn't work, etc., so whether you do it or you hire someone else, look to do some repairs in your rental units.

You will have tenant's that will constantly break things. Other problems are: clogged sinks and toilets. As long as you are not charging the tenant but you keep repairing or fixing the same problems, the tenants won't have any incentive to take better care of the apartment. So I suggest before you hand over the keys you do a walk-through of the apartment, showing and documenting, on a checklist that all toilets, sink faucets, light fixtures, heating and air conditioning units, etc. are working. I would have the tenant to sign the checklist, as well. Once the tenant moves into the apartment and you begin to get service calls, the first call would be on you as the owner and maybe the second one. But after that you should charge a fee, because if you have to call a plumber out, there is definitely going to be a charge! Even when you are doing the repairs, you might have to rent tools, this will cost you money as well as time. So I think you should charge a fair fee, depending on the job, along with the tool costs.

What I have noticed is if you charge tenants you get less calls on the same problem and people tend to be more careful, because it will cost them. So don't be afraid to charge.

I rented to a couple with children and it seemed like every month I was fixing things in their apartment. I was constantly unclogging the bathtub, sink and remounting the toilet to the floor. On average it was costing me about three hours each time. Factor in the materials, also keep a log of all work performed, this way if you are servicing that apartment unit more than average, then it is time to go up on the rent, because of on-going labor and material costs.

COST SAVING TIPS

LOW WATER PRESSURE PROBLEMS:

There might come a time when your tenants will complain that the water pressure is too low in their apartment. Before you hire a plumber to come out and fix it, first try the following things:

Find out if it is just one apartment or the whole building. If it is just one apartment, check each fixture to see which one is low on pressure, if it's the kitchen sink remove the strainer on the faucet, then turn on the water. If the water comes out strong then that was the problem. If you still have a problem, check your plumbing under the sink and in the basement to see if you have galvanized pipe or copper. If the piping is galvanized you might have to replace it with copper pipe. Then check the water pressure in the basement, if the pressure is low, check to see if the main water shut off is on all the way. It is possible that the shut off valve needs to be replaced due to corrosion. To do that you would need a plumber, or have knowledge of where the outside shut off is located. It is normally in the front of the building. Once located, remove the man-hole. The shut off to the property is probably a turn knob or a special wrench or both. If you are not sure have a professional plumber help you out. Once the water has been shut off, replace the shut off, then turn the water back on. If the water pressure is better then that was the problem, if the pressure is still low, then call your local water department to have them come out and inspect the main shut off to the building.

Those are the steps that I took. However, I did call three plumbers out to take a look. The first guy told me all the galvanized pipe going from the main shut off outside would have to be replaced and to do that he would have to get a permit, then he would dig up the yard in the front of the building, once all that was done he would replace the pipes in the basement as well. His price was between $8 to $10 thousand dollars. I would probably have paid it if I had the money. Then the second guy came out and he wanted $12 hundred dollars to dig up the front as well and put in new plumbing. I was about to give him $300 dollars good faith money to start the job, however he wasn't going to be ready to start the job for another week or so, but he still wanted the money up front. I decided against paying someone up front and then have to wait for them to get started, if ever. A lot can happen in a week or two, so he wasn't happy about my decision not to put money up until he was ready to start the job. He gave me an ultimatum, either I pay now or he was not going to do the job. So I let him walk. Here's my take on someone needing most of their money up front, it let's me know that they probably don't have credit with their suppliers and that's not the way to go. The job may never get started, or started and never finished either way it will be difficult to get your money back.

What I did do was meet the water department at my rental property and let them check it out. The first two times that they came out they said the shut off in front of the house was okay, but I knew that wasn't true because 1) there was water in the hole, and 2) I tried to turn the water off from in front of my building and it didn't work. So, when I met the water department at the building, they tried it and agreed it was the shut off in front of the building that didn't work and once the shut off was replaced the water pressure was flowing strong again.

Always call the local water department out first and try to be there when they come out. If the water department does not find a problem, then have three licensed professional plumbers come out to assess the problem and give their estimated cost for the job. You will then be more educated about possible problems and also have a comparison of prices to work with. This will stop those that would try to cheat consumers that are not familiar with industry standards.

FLUORESCENT BULBS:

Fluorescent bulbs are the way to go inside and outside of your apartments (and your personal residence) because they will save you a lot of money on the cost of electricity.

FURNISHING STOVES & REFRIGERATORS:

I used to furnish stoves and refrigerators. However these two appliances can be costly in three ways:

1) The up-keep
2) The expense to repair them
3) The time it will take to clean them, after a tenant moves out.

It is best to have the tenant furnish their own appliances.

SEPARATE HEATING BILLS:

If you can afford it, heating costs should be separate, where each tenant has their own hot water tank and furnace. I can't tell you how many times I had to pay the heating costs of my rental properties only to find out that the tenants had their windows up and guess who's money was going out the window? Mine. The tenants tell you it is too hot they open the windows to balance the heat, which can be very expensive to the owner. What I did notice once I separated the heat and the tenants were responsible for paying, they were more responsible. I did not see any windows up. Also having separate heat, I saved by not having a gas bill.

COIN OPERATED WASHER & DRYERS:

I had an old coin operated washer & dryer in one of my buildings and when they finally broke down for good, I decided to buy a non coin operated washer and dryer. My old machine didn't make a lot of money but it was convenient to use. Most of the tenants went to the laundry mat, which was okay with me, so I thought it would be the same way with the new automatic machines. Wrong!! Those machines were going day and night they were hot to the touch and if you thought that was bad enough, it wasn't, tenants were washing one pair of gym shoes in a full drum of water. I had one tenant that would let the dryer heat up for thirty minutes, then put their clothes in to dry for an additional sixty, then another sixty minutes. Can you imagine how much money I could have been made if it were a coin-operated machine? The abuse was way out of control. I even tried to set the timer for a set amount of minutes needed to dry clothes however, tenants found a way to get around that too. Then finally I put in a coin operated washing machine and the drying was free.

The abuse continued. Now tenants would wash their clothes by hand in their apartments and dry the wet clothes in the dryer, which would make the dryer work longer and harder to dry their wet clothes. So finally I just replaced the dryer too. Now the coin operated machines are seldom used.

STRESS AND RENTAL PROPERTY

Rental Property can be one of the most stressful investments because it can drain you financially, physically, as well as mentally, if you own several or more properties, and here's why. If one of the tenants fall behind on their rent payments, that is less income coming in. If you have to evict them now the apartment is tied up with no income until you go the court. If the tenant decides to get free legal help, now you have to hire an attorney to represent you for about $1,000 to $1,500 dollars, and if you are like most people you don't have money like that. You also have to pay court costs, which is around $300 - $400 dollars, in court, if you go to trial it can be dragged out as long as six months or more, all the while you are not collecting any rent. It can turn into a nightmare. On the one hand you are fighting in court to get the tenant out and on the other hand you are still trying to pay the mortgage, taxes, insurance, gas, light, water bills, etc.

What makes matters worse is when the tenant walks right past you going into the apartment knowing they haven't paid you for months. What's even more stressful is if it is winter time and you still have to heat the apartment, all the while you have to keep the heat on with no rent coming in, and when you fall behind on the mortgage the bank is threatening foreclosure. I've seen in some cases both tenants stop paying in a two flat now you have a hundred percent of no income coming in, and what makes it worse is if both tenants sue you in court with the same attorney. And don't have a house you rent out that's a hundred percent lost rent, I don't mean to sound negative it's just the truth. I've seen landlords walk away from property because of this. Getting a rental property is one thing, keeping it is another. You find yourself thinking to yourself what you could have done with the ten to twenty percent down you had to come up with along with insurance for one year to buy the property, and the money used to pay expenses when tenants stop paying or are unable to. Then comes the up keep, making sure the outside as well as the inside of the property is in good condition. And most of all managing the tenants, once new tenants move in the old one's tend to complain about things they don't like about them until everyone gets used to each other. You find yourself spending so much time fixing up and repairing the rental properties that you don't have time to work on your own place. My mother once told me I was just giving myself work to do, and boy was she right! I used to want to own one hundred apartment units and I came close to having it, but the second worst recession in the United States and the world happened in the year 2007. Banks started losing money, people were losing their homes, jobs were being lost, companies and banks were going under, it was beginning to get really bad, and I was trying my best to get this six unit apartment building. The owner was losing the property and I was trying everything to get it not knowing the economy was going to get even worst. I even tried to put my personal home up for collateral, but the banks stopped lending money, even if you had A+ credit, they still were not lending. If anything they were cutting people's lines of credit and cutting credit limits in half or cutting your credit off altogether. I was not able to get a loan and thank God for that, because things got hard for me too, my tenants started losing their jobs or being laid off, and I found myself using my savings and credit cards to pay the mortgages and keep everything going, which in one year ½ I racked up over $90,000 dollars in debt, while my places sat empty.

Lesson #1: Never use your personal home for collateral.

Lesson #2: Never use your personal savings to save a property, because a mortgage company will let you do that, and once your savings run out, you can still lose the property. And not have any savings. In my case I could have lost my home.

I have a brother two years older than me, as I was buying real estate, he was enjoying himself. He kept a new car, boat, summer home, went on trips, fixed up his home and more and all the time I thought that he was doing it wrong. When I think about it now I could have done ninety-thousand dollars worth of things differently, than waste time and money on rental property, where as like spend the money on me or my personal residence. I have owned my home for about five years and I have not been able to enjoy it or fix it up due to constantly working on and keeping the rental properties going. Between painting, repairs, eviction court, getting apartments ready for rent, sometimes I think it's easier to be a tenant than a landlord. I'm not saying all tenants are bad it's just that times have changed. For the most part, people do take pride in where they live, now a days, I find that some people just don't care because it is not their property and they feel, why should I do the extra's like clean the halls, pick up paper or shovel the snow? My advice is to invest in your home because that is where you will spend the most time. Then invest in a REIT, which stands for real estate investment trust. This is a Fund that invests solely in real estate, like shopping malls, office buildings, high rise apartment buildings and storage facilities. The good part is you buy your shares and do not have to worry about all the other responsibilities that come with rental property.

TO KEEP A TENANT OR NOT

Finding a good tenant can some time take time. By this I mean someone that will follow all or most of the rules, someone who will pay their rent on time, and not be a problem for the other tenants in the building. And when you find this particular tenant always respect and do right by them too. I don't mean constantly telling them how great they are because that can work against you too. Never let a tenant know that you need them or their money even if you do. Even though we all need money to keep things running at our rental properties, showing any sign of desperation will lead to tenants becoming lax at following the rules spelled out in their lease agreement. Things like allowing other family members to move in, getting a pet when pets are not allowed, partying as if they are the only tenants in the building, taking over the back yard, not paying late fees with the rent, etc. It is best to keep your relationship with tenants as businesslike as possible.

I had a couple that wanted to rent from me, when I spoke with the gentleman over the phone he had a very pleasant personality. When he came out to view the apartment, with his girlfriend, I thought he had a pleasant personality as well. One thing I did notice was his girlfriend didn't do a lot of talking. So, I kind of looked at other things about her that would give some insight into her personality. I tend to be a good judge of character. Even though she didn't say much, my instincts told me that she was going to be a problem. After they moved in there was a lot of company in and out of the apartment, mainly her friends. The music was loud and she let her sister move in along with five children. When I spoke with the man of the house about the situation, he assured me that the situation would get better. However, as time went on things started to get worse! His girlfriend would belittle him in to thinking like her, by making him feel that he was less of a man because he wanted to follow the rules. So, in order not to look bad in her eyesight he would ignore the rules, too. The one thing they did do well was pay the rent on time. But when you weigh the bad things against paying the rent on time, the bad things outweighed the one good thing. The final straw came when I was in their apartment adjusting the heat, and the girlfriend, her sister and another young man was sitting at the table, they appeared to be rolling cigarettes, until they asked me if I would like a hit, then I realized that it was drugs that they were smoking. I politely told them no thank you. I had been working in their apartment all day, I was tired and ready to go home. When I finally made it home and got comfortable, it hit me. It was bad enough that they were smoking marijuana, but to openly do it while the landlord was in the apartment, and with young children running around. This showed two things: 1. they didn't have respect for themselves and 2. They did not have respect for the landlord. The lease for their apartment would soon be up for renewal but I decided not to renew their lease.

Always take notes whenever you talk to your tenants about a problem and keep it in their file. This way just like in the above situation, when the tenant can't understand why they have to move, you can point out the instances where they were in non-compliance with the rules of the property, clearly stated in their lease. Eventually they did move out.

The other tenant I would like to discuss, for the most part, is a good tenant. They do follow the rules, take good care of the apartment as if it is their own, but the only problem with this particular tenant is they cannot seem to get their money in order, which if you are like the average person, you do not have money to carry the tenant that is always late.

This also causes you to be late paying the mortgage company. Even though the tenant pays late fees, as the mortgage holder, you have to pay late fees as well as other fees because of the frequent late payments. All of a sudden you start to lose money every month. And since you buy property to make money, not break even, this is unacceptable. In this case the landlord is being penalized because the tenant is being irresponsible in paying their rent. You should bring this to the tenant, in a non-threatening way of course, expressing to the tenant if things don't get better you might not renew their lease. Hopefully things will get better. If not you will have to make the decision to keep the tenant or not.

My next tenant is the type that just can't seem to keep the place clean. They usually create or bring a pest problem to the property, because of their un-cleanliness. They pay their rent on time, follow the rules but just can't get this one area in check. Keeping them could possibly infest the whole building with roaches and mice. In this case you just have to let the tenant know how you feel about the way the apartment is being kept. Because in the long run it's going to cost you in extermination fees as well as the lost of good tenants. No one in their right mind wants to live in those conditions. My advice is before a lease renewal you inspect their apartment and if things have not changed, they should not get a new lease. The tenant is now living month-to-month. If things still don't improve, it is time to ask them to move.

WHAT HAPPENS WHEN YOU FALL BEHIND ON THE MORTGAGE?

WHAT SHOULD YOU DO FIRST?

If you are like most apartment owners there will be a time when tenants don't pay and you will fall behind a month or two on the mortgage. The first thing you should do is call the mortgage company, even if you don't know when you can pay on the mortgage, they need to hear from you, be honest about your situation. The bank will try to work with you because they are in the business of making money not losing money. If it's a temporary problem, let the bank know that too. Banks have programs to help you, again they must hear from you. When I was struggling with one of my two flat properties, tenants were not paying rent. I had two choices: I could pay the mortgage and let the tenant's live for free or I could put the tenant in Eviction Court. I chose Eviction Court and that's what I explained to the mortgage company. Don't get me wrong, first and foremost the bank wants to collect their money. As long as you don't fall three months behind, you can buy yourself some time. If you live in the property, you can ask for a temporary reduction in the mortgage payment amount, say for two or six months. However, if you don't occupy the property you may want to request a traditional loan modification. Another option would be to ask if you can spread the past due balance over six months. If you spread the past due mortgage over three to six month's, be prepared to pay the past due amount along with your regular mortgage payments. This is where good bookkeeping skills come into play. You will need to gather documents like W-2's, check stubs, bank statements, leases, utility bills, etc. Most of the time if you are struggling but somehow keep current with your mortgage payments, the bank won't allow you to do a modification because they don't feel you are in need of reduced payments. **As always seek professional advice.**

EVICTION DAY

There might be a time when you will have to deal with eviction. When a tenant falls too far behind to catch themselves up and they don't want to move, you will go through the court system to have the tenant removed from the property. Not only will you pay court costs, possible attorney fees, lost rent, the cost to redecorate the apartment, etc. you now have to put the tenants belongings out too. In Illinois the County of Cook, the way it used to be is you would pay a fee and the Cook County Sheriff Deputy would meet you at the property and they would have movers take everything out of the apartment, sitting the items next to the curve. Now all they will do is post a sign on the front door of the apartment that states "No Trespassing" and if no one is home, they leave. Now you are there without security, if the tenant or tenants should walk up while you are in the process of moving them out, it can get ugly real fast. What if the person is a hot head, now you're in the middle of confusion and possibly even defending yourself in a fight with un-ruly tenants. To me that was the worst change the Sheriff Department could have made. My advice is be very particular who you rent to.

LIABILITIES OF OWNING PROPERTY

When you own property you are liable for things that happen in and around your property. You will need to inspect your property on a regular basis to make sure that you don't have anything that tenants can trip and fall over. You should also check for any unsafe conditions things that could cause harm to your tenants, such as: loose bricks, staircases with objects stored on or next to them, hanging wire, ice on the steps or ground. If these things are not corrected, your insurance company won't feel obligated to be responsible and pay off any filed claims. One of my tenants was visiting a friend and he tripped and fell because the front step had deteriorated. He is now wearing a leg cast, has hired a lawyer and is taking pictures of the step. He is in the process of suing the owner for whatever he can get. I am sure that once the smoke clears the landlord of this property would have come out cheaper had they just repaired the step. I had a similar problem with one of my concrete steps. The step deteriorated because of exposure to snow and salt. So when the tenant brought it to my attention, I immediately drove out to take a look at it and true enough one of the stairs had crumbled in the front. I told the tenant I would deal with the problem once the weather was better, since we were getting close to spring and in the month of March the weather can go either way. The tenant sent me another text stating that his daughter's friend had fallen on the step. I immediately went out to close off the area while I looked on the internet to figure out how to fix it. That is what I love about the internet anything that you need to know or have an idea how to fix, you can go to the internet for help. That is how I learned how to repair the step. It was quite easy. Had I called a contractor he would have wanted to tear down the whole porch, but by me not having a lot of money, it was more economical to repair it myself. Again if you are not sure, you should get quotes from at least three licensed contractors. You should get an explanation of the work that needs to be done and an estimate on the cost. By the time you get to the third contractor, you will be knowledgeable about the job and you will be able to discuss what you want done. Remember, if you can talk about the job, you will less likely be over charged.

VIOLATION COURT

If you thought Eviction Court was costly, sit in on Violation Court. It makes Eviction Court look like child's play. This is one place that you don't want to end up. You can be fined anywhere from $100 to $500 per day for sited violations against your property, and if there is more than one violation, the cost will be even greater. When I was summoned to appear in Violations Court, it was because my tenant refused to transfer gas service to his name, I eventually had to have it disconnected, once removed from my name. This tenant sat in a cold apartment in the heart of winter. He became frustrated and called the City on me. Had I lost this case in Violation Court, I would have been fined up to $2,500 for not supplying heat to his apartment. That is why it is very important to keep your place in good working condition and keep a paper trail of all agreements as to if the tenant or you will pay for heat and electricity service. It is also important never to have wire hanging, faulty electrical and plumbing, unsafe porches, stairs and sidewalks. Never let tenants store anything in walk areas where others can easily trip over them. This is also a fire hazard. Remember, the Landlord is liable if someone hurts themselves on your property. Always keep working smoke detectors, carbon-monoxide detectors and fire extinguishers hung in all apartments. If you do these things you should be able to avoid ending up in Violations Court.

THE AWARD SEEKING TENANT

Some tenant's feel when they pay their rent that they are doing you a favor. What they don't understand is if the landlord doesn't pay the mortgages, with their rent payments, they won't have a roof over their heads. Also, if the utility company is not paid, they will not have water, heat, etc. Some tenant's will tell you "I paid my rent". But isn't that what they are supposed to do? You cannot live anywhere for free. When I pay the mortgage, the bank doesn't reward me at the end of the year for being responsible and paying the mortgage. They feel that if I want to keep the place, I will pay the mortgage.

FINAL WORDS

I hope that this book was informative. It was not written to discourage or encourage you. It was written to help you decide if being a landlord is really for you. Good Luck!